ST. LOUIS

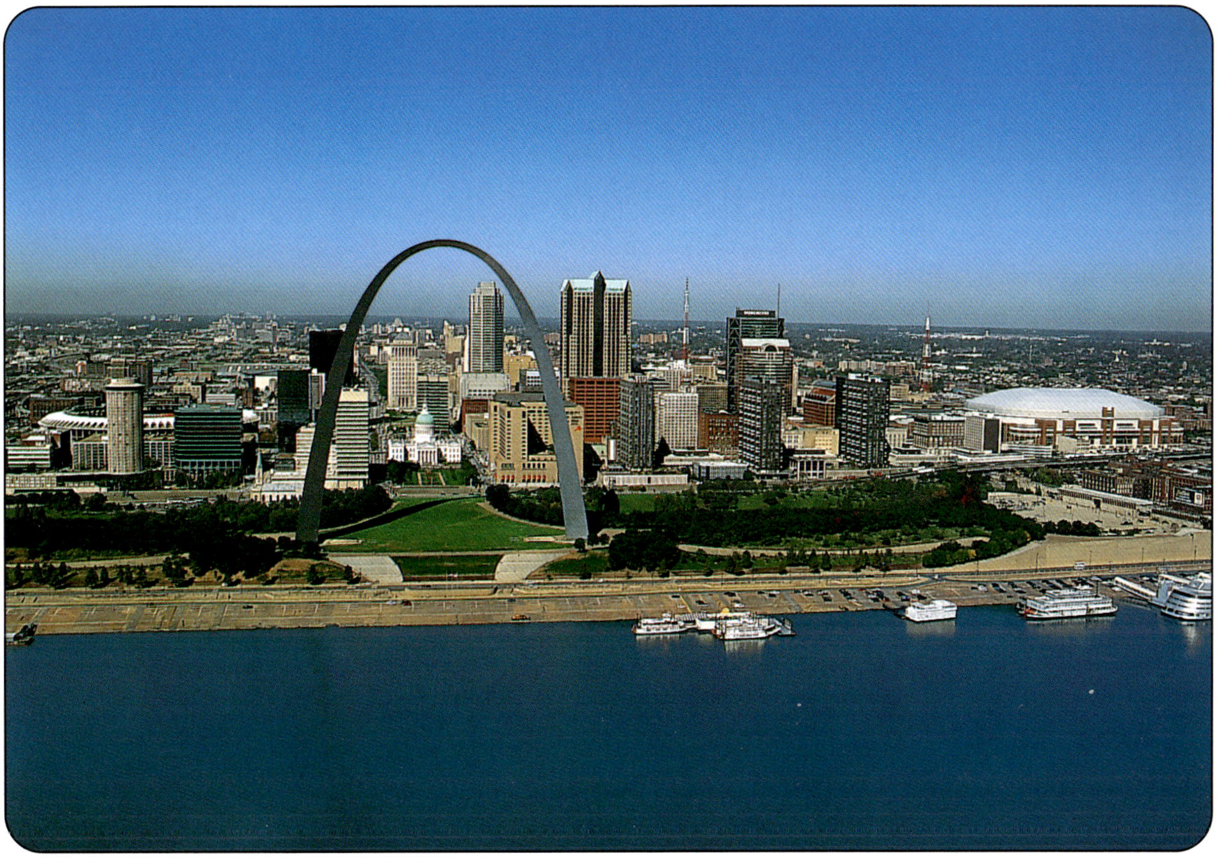

Photos by
ANDREA PISTOLESI

ST. LOUIS

Publication created and designed by Casa Editrice Bonechi
Publication Manager: Monica Bonechi
Project and graphic realisation: Sonia Gottardo
Picture research: Monica Bonechi
New edition revised by Silvano Domestici
Editing: Simonetta Giorgi

Text: Rosanna Cirigliano

© Copyright
CASA EDITRICE BONECHI
Via Cairoli 18/b -50131 Florence - Italy

e-mail:bonechi@bonechi.it
Internet:www.bonechi.it

ISBN 978-88-8029-649-2

All rights reserved.
Reproduction even in part forbidden.

Printed in Italy by
Centro Stampa Editoriale Bonechi.

Photographs from the Archives of
Casa Editrice Bonechi *taken by*
Andrea Pistolesi

Photographs kindly provided by Joe Luman:
cover; pages 1, 7, 12, 14, 15, 23

The cover, layout and artwork by the Casa Editrice Bonechi
graphic artists in this publication are protected
by international copyright.

ISBN 1-56274-418-6

* * *

MEET ME IN ST. LOUIS

St. Louis is at a crossroads. The city that the in-flight magazine of TWA, *Ambassador*, characterized as "the heart of the heart of the country", is shedding its former image of an old industrial city to reveal a revitalized metropolitan center which attracts tourists for business and pleasure.
This change began in the 1970s, when the city started transforming existing resources, and continued to the 1980s. A former 19th century warehouse district was carefully restored to house a variety of restaurants, clubs, and shops, and dubbed **Laclède's Landing** in honor of the founder of St. Louis. The closed railroad terminal, **Union Station,** became a festival marketplace. At the same time, new ideas were developed, which led to the construction of the **A.J. Cervantes Convention Center.** Suddenly, St. Louis became a popular place for many groups to hold meetings and conferences, so much so that the Convention Center has been expanded to contain five exhibit halls; This in turn
influenced the hotel industry to open 5,000 new rooms between 1985 and 1990, and there was a dramatic increase in the number of downtown restaurants. More shopping malls were built, including the *St. Louis Centre,* the largest enclosed downtown shopping mall in the country; also in the area is the *St. Louis Galleria.*
Historically speaking, St. Louis has always been at a crossroads. Located 10 miles south of the confluence of the Mississippi and Missouri rivers, it was founded as a center for French fur trade, ceded to Spain, and finally sold to the United States.
Intrepid pioneers coming from the East often considered the city as the **Gateway to the West.** Their number included Lewis and Clark, whose expedition was only one of many starting from this area of eastern Missouri situated on the western bank of the Mississippi River across from Illinois. Steamboats were at the center of thriving commercial activity which linked the four corners of the United States between 1817 and 1870. During the Civil War, natives supported the Union cause, although a pro-Southern sentiment did exist among some. But, like it or not, the city served as a supply base and hospital center for the North under martial law. After hostilities ceased, river trade gradually gave way to

The Meeting of the Rivers Fountain.

railroad transport, and St. Louis became an important hub in that nationwide system. Czech, Irish, Italian, and especially German immigrants continued to arrive in the city in droves, influencing the local culture. The first kindergarten in the United States (1873) was founded in St. Louis, and an enterprising immigrant named Eberhard Anheuser re-opened a failing brewery, later forming a partnership with his son-in-law, Adolphus Busch. They invented a name for their beer – Budweiser – because it "sounded" German, and was easy to pronounce. Ditto for their premium product, Michelob.

Moving to the 20th century, 1904 marks an important date in St. Louis history. The Olympic games were held in the city that year, the first time ever in the United States. That was also the year of the Louisiana Purchase Exposition, better known as the St. Louis World's Fair, hosted in

Forest Park, and famous for its display of technological developments. The World's Fair also has a claim to fame for popularizing the first fast-food – hot dogs, hamburgers, iced tea, and ice cream cones. St. Louis became important as a center for shoe manufacturing, which it is no longer, and for retail and wholesale sales. During World War II, while many servicemen passed through Union Station, the McDonnell Aircraft Corporation, headquartered locally, developed the first jet-propelled fighter, the McDonnell Phantom. This gave rise to a thriving local aircraft industry, which was flanked by car manufacture. General Motors, Ford, and Chrysler all operate plants in the area, which is second only to Detroit in automobile production.
St. Louis' central location makes it easy to reach by plane, train, or bus.

The Eads Bridge is the oldest St. Louis bridge spanning the Mississippi.

The silver ribbon known as the Gateway Arch.

SHOWBOAT

*I do not know much about gods; but I think that the river
Is a strong brown god – sullen, untamed and intractable,
Patient to some degree, at first recognized as a frontier;
Useful, untrustworthy, as a conveyor of commerce;
Then only a problem confronting the builder of bridges.
The problem once solved, the brown god is almost forgotten
By the dwellers in cities – ever, however, implacable,
Keeping his seasons and rages, destroyer, reminder
Of what men choose to forget.*

T.S. ELIOT
from FOUR QUARTETS

Most artists work from first-hand experience, turning the obvious into pure gold. Poet T.S. Eliot was no exception. In the case of the above poem, he was specifically talking about the Mississippi River. Later a British citizen, T.S. Eliot was born and raised in St. Louis. About the Mississippi, he said it all.

St. Louis is spread along 19 miles of the Mississippi river shoreline. The river is spanned by a number of bridges, including the MacArthur, the Chain of the Rocks, McKinley, Jefferson Barracks, Clark, Veterans Memorial, and Poplar Street, all of steel construction. The oldest and most well-known is the **Eads Bridge** (1874), pictured above, to the side, and on the following page. Designated a National Historic Landmark, it was the world's first steel-truss span.

As for the the historic paddlewheelers, or replicas thereof, several are docked along the St. Louis riverfront. The steamboats have met various fates. Mississippi river cruises can be taken on the **Belle of St. Louis** (including a moonlight cruise), the **Huck Finn**, the **Becky Thatcher**, and the **Tom Sawyer**. (T.S. Eliot was not the only

Another view of the Eads Bridge.

Historic steamboats are still docked at St. Louis, in the shadow of the Gateway Arch. Cruises of the Mississippi can be taken aboard some of these riverboats; dinner theatre is available on others.

writer who recorded impressions of the Mississippi; let's not forget Samuel Clemens, alias Mark Twain, whose first book was *Life On the Mississippi*).

Tugboats still push barges past St. Louis, which remains the country's second busiest inland port, with service to Minneapolis-St. Paul to the north, New Orleans to the south, and connections to 27 other metropolitan areas. As a means of practical transportation, however, river travel has been superseded by air travel. **The Lambert-St. Louis International Airport** is the seventh busiest in the nation, and can be reached 24 hours a day by bus, taxi, or airport limousine.

Locally, this excellent network obviously has had its impact in commercial terms. St. Louis is the headquarters for 10 of the Fortune 500 companies. The original McDonnell Aircraft Corporation, previously mentioned, evolved to meet the needs of the space age, to produce Mercury, the space capsule in which John Glenn orbited the Earth, and later, Skylab. In 1967, it merged with Douglas Aircraft to form the **McDonnell-Douglas Corporation,** a major supplier of jet fighters to the armed forces. Similarly, **General Dynamics** makes aircraft, missiles, ships, submarines, and electronic equipment. **Monsanto,** a giant in the chemical industry, has diversified product lines which include pharmaceuticals. Home appliances and power tools are the speciality of **Emerson Electric,** and pet food is the domain of **Ralston Purina.**

Beer, already touched upon, is another subject dear to St. Louis, and will be more fully examined, as appropriate, in the sports section titled *Batter's Up.*

Oh, yes, the river. It flows on, continually changing yet always the same.

The Arch is spectacular from every point of view.

THE SPIRIT OF ST. LOUIS

In 1927, a group of St. Louis businessmen decided to give financial backing to the first solo transatlantic plane flight from New York to Paris. They saw it as the conquest of a new frontier. As luck would have it, their support of the initiative turned out to be a fantastic piece of advertising for that basic philosophy of enterprise which underlies the city itself. The pilot was Charles Lindbergh, who dubbed his plane "The Spirit of St. Louis".

"The Spirit of St. Louis". Nowhere is it better exemplified than in the silver ribbon known as the **Gateway Arch.** In 1990, the Gateway Arch turned 25. Its history, however, reaches back to Thomas Jefferson, our third president, who authorized the Louisiana Purchase from Napoleon in 1803, thus doubling the area of the United States. This act unleashed exploration of the West and the massive pioneer movement which lasted throughout the entire century. Many brave settlers used the strategic position of St. Louis as their starting point, or at least as a place to rest and restock provisions. Hence the nickname "Gateway to the West", a homage to the conquest of the old frontier.

In memory of these events, President Franklin Roosevelt declared the land where the future Arch would stand a National Historic Site in 1935. The urban riverfront park was named the Jefferson National Expansion Memorial, and a competition launched for an appropriate monument. Architect Eero Saarinen won in 1947. His design was breathtaking: a steel, inverted, three-sided catenary curve, 630 feet high. Actual construction on the Arch started in 1963, and it was completed in 1965. Unfortunately, Saarinen did not live to see his Arch; he died in 1961.

The Gateway Arch is hollow, and visitors may ride up to a special enclosed viewing deck which affords a spectacular view and where, on a windy day, the sway of the Arch can be felt. Beneath the Arch, the **Museum of Westward Expansion** (open 8 am to 10 pm Memorial Day through Labor Day; 9 am to 6 pm the rest of the year) narrates the

The Old Cathedral is St. Louis' oldest house of worship.

story of the pioneers and of their migration to the West. A movie retraces the Lewis and Clark Expedition from St. Louis to the Pacific. Another documentary narrates the building of the Arch, filmed while work was in progress.

On the riverfront, the Gateway Arch stands on its own, unencumbered, a poetic statement of what St. Louis is all about.

Close to the Arch on Walnut Street stands the **Basilica of St. Louis, King of France,** familiarly known as the **Old Cathedral.** Built in a vaguely Neoclassical or Greek Revival style (apart from the steeple) between 1831 and 1834, the Old Cathedral, as its name implies, was St. Louis' first cathedral, and is the oldest west of the Mississippi. Pope John XXIII conferred basilica status on the Catholic house of worship in 1961, and President John Kennedy designated it a National Monument. The Cathedral can be visited daily from 10 am to 5 pm, 10 am to 8 pm in the summer, along with the Cathedral museum on the west side of the church which contains the tomb of the first Bishop of St. Louis, the original church bell, and other objects of interest.

The transition from spiritual to temporal is a matter of a short walk to a district known as **Laclède's Landing,** (following page) between the Eads and King bridges just north of the Gateway Arch. This nine-block neighborhood on the riverfront was part of the French fur trading village (hence its name) which was to become modern-day St. Louis, and which is the last remaining example in the city of the original street layout. The streets themselves are paved in cobblestone, patrolled by an occasional policeman on horseback, and illuminated by wrought-iron lamps. Nineteenth-century brick buildings (formerly warehouses) have been converted into small shops and boutiques, galleries, offices, unusual restaurants, and a collection of lively nightspots which serve liquor until two in the morning.

Invariably, inside these pubs and cafes, music is to be heard. It is probably *jazz*. Jazz was born along the Mississippi River out of ragtime, blues, Louisiana Creole dance tunes, Black spirituals, revival meeting hymns, and work songs. Jazz has a smokey, hot sound, suited to late nights and

Laclède's Landing recreates the atmosphere of Old St. Louis.

hard drinking – and pure enjoyment. It has bounce and beat because it is syncopated music. The heart of jazz is improvisation. With no forethought, the musician plays on-the-spot variations on a theme, or takes a theme into a new form, and only he is aware of what he is doing and where he is going. This is the opposite philosophy to that of a a pre-planned variation. *Let the good times roll!* Put together a trumpet, trombone, sax, clarinet, bass, and drums, and there are the basic components of a jazz band. What happens next is anyone's guess.

Oh, yes, blues. In 1914, a musician named W.C. Handy wrote and published the composition that would make him famous, *The St. Louis Blues.* Blues is a slow kind of song that was later woven into jazz music. Blues were made up and sung by Blacks in the fields and cities of the South as folk songs. Feeling "blue" means feeling sad, so the words of blues songs expressed the collective emotions of the singers at the time. Perfect pitch is not important in blues; the singer often wavers around the tone according to his feeling. As for W.C. Handy, he was born in Alabama and later came to St. Louis with other musicians in a quartet. They saw hard times, and Handy left the city for Memphis, where he would later draw on his experiences to compose *The St. Louis Blues.* Handy was the first to write blues down, and for this he is known as "the father of the blues".

What is actually popular in St. Louis now is *ragtime.* Ragtime is a style of piano jazz that was played in honky-tonk cafés in the 1890s. It grew out of the banjo solos of minstrel shows. Piano players would imitate the jangling sound of banjos using fast, strongly accented, syncopated patterns over a steady strong beat kept by the left hand. This made for the familiar jerky rhythms popularized by Texan Scott Joplin (1869-1917) in his 39 piano rags. Ragtime was used to accompany silent movies, but by the end of World War II, it was swept aside for the jazz combo, although it has enjoyed revivals from time to time. St. Louis hosts a **National Ragtime and Classic Jazz Festival** for five days every June.

Busch Stadium, home of the St. Louis Cardinals.

BATTER'S UP

St. Louis is a sports-crazy town, and much of the country is crazy about St. Louis sports. First and foremost, this means National League baseball, played in the beautiful, circular **Busch Stadium** (completed in 1966) at Walnut, Broadway, Spruce and 7th St. There, some 54,000 fans have an unobstructed view of exciting home games played by the **St. Louis Cardinals.** During the 1980s alone, the Cardinals won three pennants and one World Series Championship (1982). Overall, they have won nine World Series Championships, obliterating the memory of the ill-fated St. Louis Browns baseball team, who left town in the 1950s to become the Baltimore Orioles. Perhaps the most famous Cardinal is Stan "the Man" Musial. From 1941 to the early 1960s, this gentleman and consummate sportsman played his entire career in St. Louis, knocking in a career total of 3,630 hits for a career batting average of 331. He was named Most Valuable Player three times. A native of Pennsylvania, "the Man's" roots have all but been forgotten, as he remains highly visible in St. Louis for his business and civic endeavors.

Naturally, Musial has been named to the Baseball Hall of Fame, along with 27 other Cards, including Dizzy Dean, Bob Gibson, and Lou Brock.

Busch Stadium is also home to the St. Louis Sports Hall of Fame, which can be visited from March to December from 10 am to 5 pm, until 11 pm on game nights; during January and February it is necessary to call for hours. It is a live action museum of St. Louis sports history which offers World Series movies, trophies, and displays, as well as movies on locally played baseball, football, basketball, hockey, golf, bowling, and soccer.

Appropriately, as may have been guessed, the local Busch family of Anheuser-Busch beer fame are the owners of the St. Louis Cardinals.

However, there is more to the St. Louis sports scene than meets the eye. A winged quarter note is the symbol of the **St. Louis Blues** hockey team.

Tennis fans may be interested to learn that St. Louis native Dwight Davis donated the Davis Cup Trophy to the sport, and Wimbledon and U.S. Open champion Jimmy Connors hails from the St. Louis area, and trained here. Ditto for Olympic runner Craig Virgin, World Heavy Boxing Champions Michael and Leon Spinks, and baseball's Yogi Berra! St. Louis-born George H. Walker put up the Walker Cup as the prize in a biannual competition between American and British golfers, and Hale Irwin is a local golfer who made good – with three U.S. Open golf championships.

Have we left something out? Bowling? That's here too, with the **National Bowling Hall of Fame** located across the street from Busch Stadium.

New monuments outside Busch Stadium. The TWA Dome, home of St. Louis Rams NFL and the Kiel Center, home of St. Louis Blues Hockey.

The Old Courthouse was the site of a trial which was instrumental in galvanizing opinion on the slavery issue.

ST. LOUIS BLUES

Part of the Jefferson National Expansion Memorial is the **Old Courthouse** at 11 North 4th St. Construction began on this graceful, harmonious building in 1839, and was completed in 1864. The architectural style is Greek Revival, as befits justice, and the Courthouse was topped in 1863 by an Italian Renaissance-style cupola, the first cast-iron dome ever built.

Was justice always rendered at the Old Courthouse? Yes and no. Slave auctions were held on its steps. But, it was also the scene of the Dred Scott trial. In 1847, Dred Scott and his wife, slaves, sued for freedom since their master had taken them to live in the Illinois and Wisconsin Territory where slavery was forbidden. They won the case, but the decision was later overturned by the U.S. Supreme Court, which moved the U.S. toward the Civil War. Dred Scott's master decided to free the slaves himself, and the papers were signed in the Old Courthouse in 1857. Sadly, Scott died the next year.

Inside, murals by Carl Wimar adorn the walls of the Old Courthouse. Museum galleries featuring exhibits on St. Louis history are open to the public, as are two restored courtrooms where great lawyers like Thomas Hart Benton fought their cases. It is open daily from 8 am to 4:30 pm. Before the Courthouse are the **Kiener Plaza Fountains,** with the statue of "The Runner" in the center. One block west is the terra cotta-colored **Wainwright Building,** a 10-story high-rise designed by Louis Sullivan and completed in 1891. The lovely structure had a vital influence on all skyscraper architecture. Its lightweight steel skeleton construction allowed for bigger windows than formerly possible.

The press, too, often has a vital influence on local and national affairs, and this can be seen with the local **St. Louis Post-Dispatch,** one of the most prestigious newspapers in the United States. The St. Louis Post-Dispatch has a long and glorious history. It was founded in 1878, when Joseph Pulitzer purchased the bankrupt St. Louis Dispatch and merged it with the St. Louis Post.

The Old Courthouse.

Pulitzer established an independent liberal policy right from the start, and took a strong stand against corruption in public office. The paper published sensational exposés, and attracted a growing readership. Meanwhile, Pulitzer endowed the Pulitzer Prizes in journalism, letters, and music in a bequest to Columbia University; the prizes are awarded annually by the president of that university on the recommendation of the Pulitzer Prize Board. Joseph Pulitzer II took control of the Post, or *the P-D*, as it was widely known, in 1911 upon his father's death. He in turn was succeeded as publisher in 1955 by Joseph Pulitzer III, who greatly improved the newspaper's international coverage. Today, the Post-Dispatch has a daily readership of 400,000 and 560,000 on Sunday. A traditional evening paper, the Post recently switched to coming out in the mornings. Its stance has moved from liberal to center, and the paper's strength lies in its excellent investigative reporting.

If live music and theatre are of interest, St. Louis has plenty to offer. First and foremost is the **St. Louis Symphony Orchestra,** conducted by maestro Leonard Slatkin. Of world renown, the St. Louis Symphony Orchestra is the second oldest symphony orchestra in the United States, founded in 1880. Musicians such as Yo Yo Ma, Isaac Stern, Itzhak Perlman and Marilyn Horne have performed with the orchestra at Powell Symphony Hall, 718 North Grand Boulevard.

In July and August, the orchestra gives the Summer *Queeny Pops Series*, performing popular music at the Greensfelder Recreation Center. Theatre and music blend in the productions given by the **Opera Theatre of St. Louis** at the Loretto Hilton Center. Classic and modern opera are all sung in English. The **St. Louis Conservatory for the Arts (CASA)** also sponsors concerts, recitals, opera, and jazz performances.

There is a lot to choose from even in just straight theater. **The Repertory Theatre of St. Louis,** 130 Edgar Road, seeks some of the finest artists in American theatre for classics, modern plays, drama, and comedy, and performances take place between September and April. **The Theatre Project Company,** 4219 Laclede, produces off-Broadway plays, and is dedicated to the employment of area theatre artists and the revitalization of St. Louis. The **Black Repertory**

The fountains of Kiener Plaza provide an impressive introduction to the Old Courthouse. The statue in the middle is "The Runner".

Company – 23rd Street Theatre (2240 St. Louis Avenue) sponsors a wide range of stage productions.

On a lighter note, St. Louis is also known for its festivals and ethnic neighborhood celebrations. Immediately, this brings to mind the **Veiled Prophet Fair.** Every July, His Majesty, the Veiled Prophet of Khorassan, sojourns in St. Louis, his favorite city. His arrival is hailed with pomp and circumstance, meaning parades, music, food, crafts, and entertainment, capped off by brilliant fireworks over the Mississippi River on the evening of the Fourth of July. The Veiled Prophet Fair was started in 1878 by a group of local businessmen who adopted a character invented by Irish poet Thomas Moore. Thankfully, the Veiled Prophet decided to return the favor by adopting St. Louis.

In keeping with the same spirit is the annual **St. Louis Storytelling Festival,** a gathering of traditional and professional storytellers held every May. The public is also invited to participate with their yarns. Moving down to the river, the Huck Finn and Tom Sawyer riverboats compete in an annual **Memorial Day Riverboat Race,** a colorful, exciting affair which is matched in the sky by the **Hot Air Balloon Race** every July. The latter attracts professional balloonists from around the country. A more sedate affair is September's **St. Louis National Charity Horse Show** at Queeny Park. This features equestrian competition by hunter, jumper, saddle, and Arabian horses.

Far Eastern culture is highlighted in the **Japanese Festival** (late July – early September) held in the Missouri Botanical Garden. And the large community of German-Americans celebrate the **St. Louis Strassenfest** (July) at West Port Plaza, and there's always plenty of bratwurst, pretzels, and other German food and drink.

And this is a return to the subject of beer. A tour of the **Anheuser-Busch Brewery** (Broadway and Pestalozzi) is recommended. See the 1892 brewhouse, inside and out, the bottling plant, and sample some of the product. Also on hand are the Clydesdale horses, originally a gift from August Busch Jr. to his father, marking the end of Prohibition. More Clydesdales can be seen at another Anheuser-Busch property, **Grant's Farm,** 10501 Gravois. As its name implies, the property once belonged to our 18th president, Ulysses S. Grant. At Grant's Farm, a trackless train carries visitors through the game preserve and past Grant's Cabin, built by Grant in 1856. The recreation area is dedicated to animals: the Clydesdales are bred and stabled here, there is a miniature zoo, and a small animal feeding area. A collection of old horse-drawn carriages and sleighs are also on display. Sleighs? Yes, it does occasionally snow in St. Louis. And this opens the door to the subject of weather.

Natives of St. Louis know well that the two most beautiful months of the year are May and October. There are four distinct seasons; while it is very cold in the winter (average snowfall – 17 inches), it is very hot and humid in the summer. Between these extremes are fairly temperate months, with random thunderstorms which should not be enough to impede a stroll down... Market Street.

The view down Market Street and the Civil Court. Building with the Gateway Arch in the background.

Another view of the Civil Courts Building seen from Memorial Plaza.

A STROLL DOWN MARKET STREET

After a visit to the Old Courthouse, a leisurely walk down scenic Market Street reveals some of St. Louis' more interesting sights. This busy artery passes through the centuries of the city's history and the changes in architectural style follow one another from the early nineteenth-century courthouse toward the monuments of the Twentieth Century. St. Louis has always been known for its fabulous architecture and it is easy to see why. Buildings and skyscrapers in every imaginable form, from Greek and Gothic Revival to Art Deco styles house the many shops and offices along the thoroughfare.

A number of surprises await near the intersection of Market and Tucker Memorial Boulevard (Twelfth Street). On the northeast corner is the impressive **Civil Courts Building** and, across the street, on the northwest corner, the splendid **Soldiers' Memorial** sits in majesty solemnity surrounded by the tranquil sea of its landscaped grounds. Just across from the Soldiers' Memorial is the **City Hall,** vested in Old World dignity, and the **Kiel Municipal Auditorium.** Only a couple more blocks down the street is **Union Station,** formerly the famous railroad station and hub of westward travel, now a luxurious hotel and shopping center. Setting the stage for the "medieval chateau" of Union Station is the brilliant **Meeting of the Waters Fountain.**

The **Civil Courts Building** towers above this stretch of Market Street with a sense of eternal authority lent to it by its mixture of modern and classical architectural styles. The sculpted relief decorating the entryway is reminiscent of the entrance to a Greek temple. Moreover, the Greek style colonnade high atop the solid modern tower serves to further accentuate the building's refined elegance.

The monumental **Soldiers' Memorial** was dedicated in 1936 to commemorate the veterans of St. Louis and those brave citizens who lost their lives in the war. The massive memorial with its

The Soldiers' Memorial is dedicated to the memory of St. Louis' veterans and war dead.

highly stylized façade and its imposing sculptures flanking the entrance, statues of mythological winged horses and an ancient warrior, not to mention the vigilant eye of the American eagle, all add poetically to the impression of the structure as a temple to sobriety. The memorial building also houses the city's military museum (open daily from 9 am to 4:30 pm, admission is free). Among the museum's many exhibits which trace the role of the city and its citizens in America's wars, are interesting displays of uniforms, period photographs, weaponry through the years, war souvenirs, and various regalia. Surrounding the memorial building and the museum is the beautiful Memorial Park, an island of grass and trees in the heart of the city that stretches along Market Street from Tucker Boulevard to 21st Street; that is, from the **Soldiers' Memorial** to the **Meeting of the Waters Fountain.** Across from the Soldiers' Memorial is the city hall of Paris. No, not really. It is, in fact, the **City Hall of St. Louis,** built to resemble its Parisian counterpart. Inside this seeming

The St. Louis City Hall, modelled after the Hotel de Ville of Paris.

*The Fox Theatre.
View of the Neoclassical Masonic Temple.
Following pages:
the busy thoroughfare of Market Street from Union Station to the river.*

sixteenth-century hotel lies the heart of St. Louis' municipal government. First incorporated as a town on November 9, 1809, St. Louis was elevated to city status by a special legislative charter in 1823. The city government was separated from that of the county of St. Louis by a provision of the 1875 state constitution; in more recent years, this has limited the boundaries of the city government with the result that only a fraction of the St. Louis area's 1.2 million inhabitants actually live in St. Louis proper. The current city government system was instituted in 1914 and consists of the familiar mayor-city council form.
While on the subject of unusual buildings, inspect St. Louis' **Masonic Temple.** Located not too far away on Lindell Boulevard is this marvelous example of architectural eccentricity: the colonnade on the entrance is clearly of Greco-Roman inspiration, but is capped by a row of Deco reliefs, all surmounted by the façade of an Ionic temple.

Just down the street from City Hall is one of the marvels of American architecture, the fabulously eclectic **Union Station,** designed by architect Theodore Link. The beautiful railway terminal that looks more like a Romanesque-style castle than a train station opened in 1894 and was once the busiest in the nation. As the covered wagons of the early pioneers faded into the pages of the History books, the way to the American West was paved with steel rails and Union Station became the real *Gateway to the West.* St. Louis, always the hub of westward expansion, became the center of rail travel and the essential link between New York and San Francisco, as depicted in the beautiful Art Nouveau stained-glass window in the station's Grand Hall. In the age of the airplane and jet-fast transportation, though, rail travel has declined and Union Station saw its last train leave in 1979. It soon lay virtually deserted. However, thanks to a massive $135 million restoration project, the station lives again. Just as in days

Looking like a medieval fortress, Union Station is now a sumptuous hotel and shopping center.

Carl Milles' "Meeting of the Waters" fountain sets the stage for Union Station.

Following pages: fabulous Union Station is a bustling center of commercial activity, its waiting room now the lounge of the Hyatt Regency Hotel.

gone by when the railroad station was the heart of the city, the new Union Station complex occupies a position of similar importance. The Grand Hall, the centerpiece of the renovation work, is now the lobby of the posh Hyatt Regency Hotel, housed in the building. The former terminal is also home to a surprising variety of unique boutiques and shops as well as a Biergarten on the shore of a lake under the old trainshed. In keeping with its new role as heart of the city, Union Station offers the chance to shop for St. Louis souvenirs, listen to some good music, or even see a film at the station's ten-screen movie theater.

Outside Union Station, there is a wonderful view of the **Meeting of the Waters Fountain** in front of the station and the city scenery of Market Street looking back toward the Old Courthouse and the Gateway Arch. The fountain in the center of Aloe Plaza was created by sculptor Carl Milles and was first unveiled in 1941. The mythic figures cast in bronze and the numerous lighted jets of water combine to form an eloquent portrayal of the meeting of the Missouri and Mississippi rivers just north of the city. In fact, throughout the city's history, the confluence of these two rivers has been of extreme importance. After all, without its fortunate geographical position, St. Louis would never have been built: its French founders were looking for a site to build a trading post and what better place than the meeting point of two great waterways. Pierre Laclède, a French merchant from New Orleans whose company had been granted exclusive rights to trade with the Indians of the region, was looking for a base of operations for expansion west of the Mississippi. In 1764, Laclède and his fourteen-year-old stepson led an expedition up the Mississippi. They chose the site of what would become St. Louis and landed there on February 14, 1764. The next day they gave the

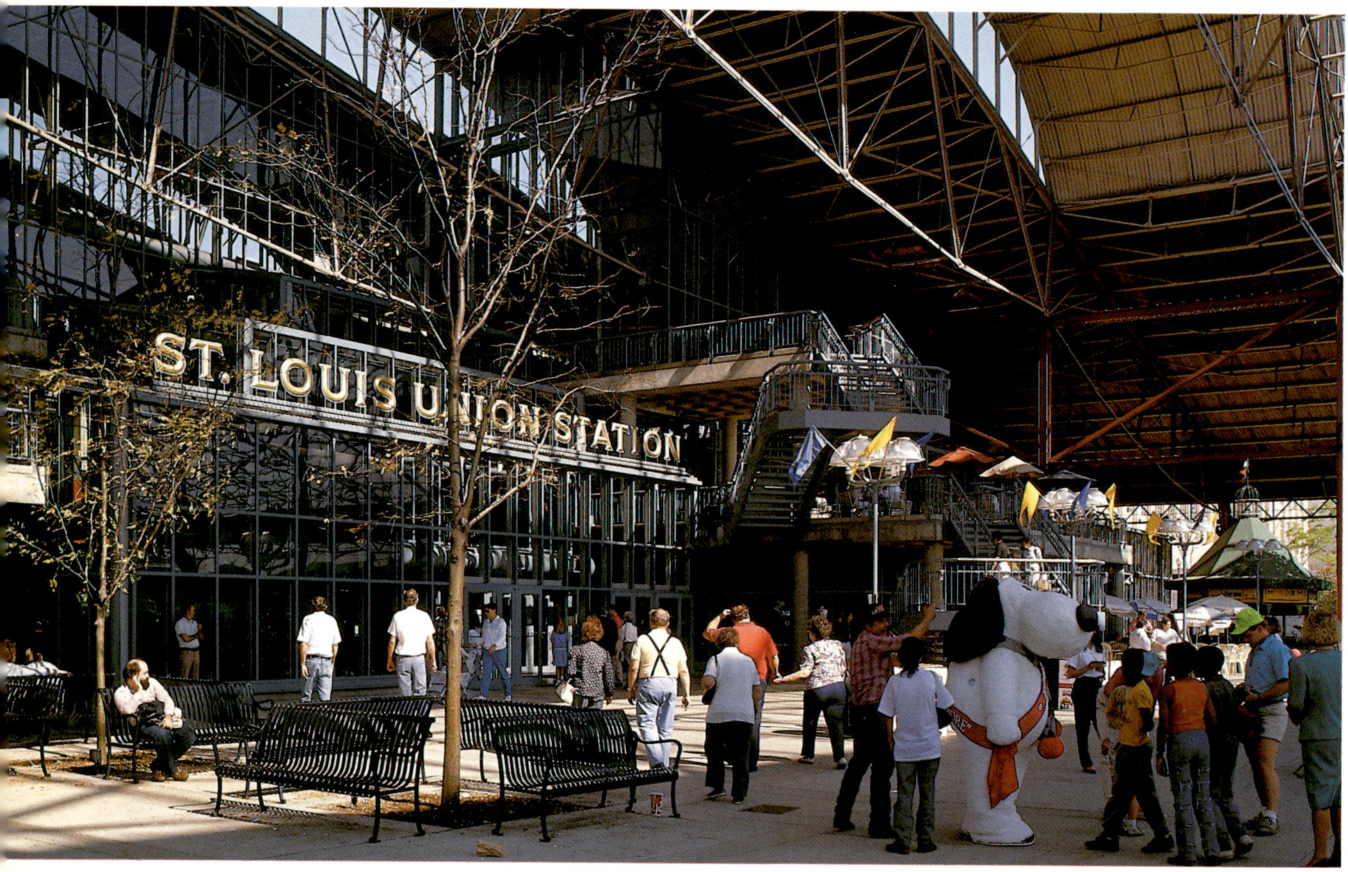
ST. LOUIS UNION STATION

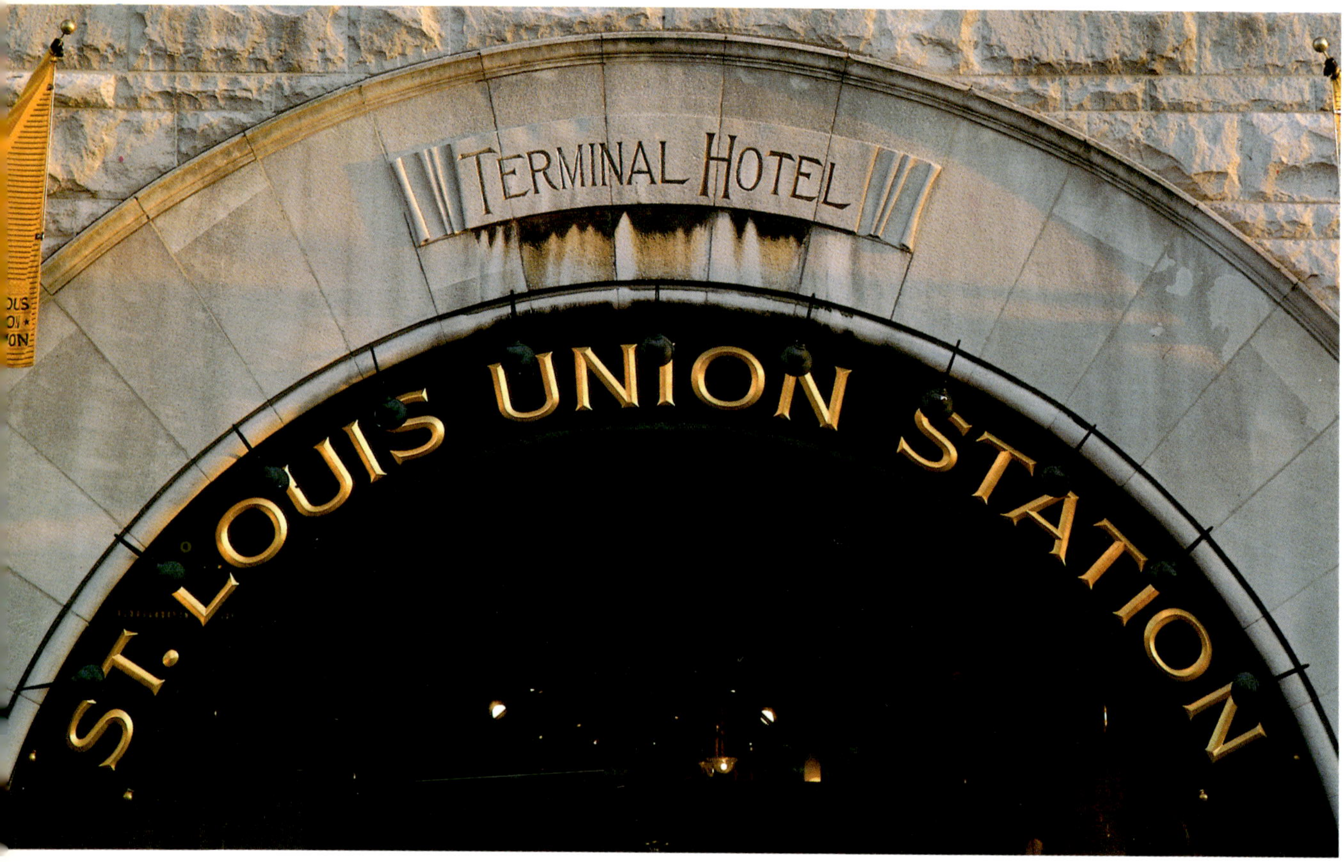
TERMINAL HOTEL
ST. LOUIS UNION STATION

Two views of Carl Milles' "Meeting of the Waters" fountain.

Following pages: the lighted jets of the "Meeting of the Waters" fill the air in Aloe Plaza.

order for their 30-man crew to begin work on the village's first buildings. When Fort Chartres on the Illinois side of the river passed into British hands in 1765 in accordance with a treaty transferring all French territory east of the Mississippi to the British, many French and French Canadians moved west to Laclède's village, preferring that to living under British rule. In 1770, a Spanish lieutenant governor arrived in St. Louis, bearing news of the secret Treaty of Fontainebleau (1762-1763), transferring the Louisiana territory to Spain. The city became the Spanish capital of Upper Louisiana and by 1772 had reached a less-than-astounding population of 399 free men and 198 slaves. The territory was regained by France in 1800, but as everyone knows, it was destined to be bought by the then-young United States in 1803. In large part due to its strategic location for river transportation, St. Louis became the seat of government for the district of Louisiana and, from 1812 to 1821, the capital of the territory of Missouri. In 1821, the year of Missouri's statehood, St. Louis had reached the relatively large population of 5,600. In the early years, the city's position was exploited mainly by fur traders; expeditions west of the Mississippi could easily be made along the Missouri River, and the furs could then be taken down the Mississippi to the thriving market of New Orleans. Goods to be sold in Missouri were brought up from New Orleans on the return trip. The invention of the steamboat, though, added a whole new dimension to commerce. The first paddle-wheel steamboat arrived in 1817 and St. Louis began its long career as a center of transportation. By the 1850s, 5,000 steamboats would land in St. Louis each year, shipping freight along the two rivers.

A little further away from the center of downtown St. Louis are a number of other sights that are not

The St. Louis Cathedral.

The St. Louis Cathedral, or New Cathedral, houses the world's largest collection of mural mosaics.

to be missed. The first of these is the **Cathedral of St. Louis,** also known as the **New Cathedral** on Lindell Boulevard at the corner of Newstead Avenue. This cathedral, the Mother Church of the Archdiocese, is an impressive blend of architectural styles and artistic beauty which exudes an immense sense of grandeur. The cathedral, begun in 1907, was dedicated in 1914. On the exterior, the church is built in the Romanesque style, reminiscent of the early medieval churches of western Europe. The interior, however, echoes the awe-inspiring beauty of a Byzantine basilica, bringing to mind the fabulous churches of Greece and the eastern Mediterranean. Inside the church, the most striking feature is the series of domes that constitute the church's nave, and in keeping with the Byzantine style, each of these domes, as well as the ceilings, the arches, and many of the wall panels, is covered with mosaics. In fact, the mosaics, executed according to medieval Byzantine style, when taken all together, add up to the largest collection of mosaics in one single site in the whole world. The beauty of the cathedral is completed by the use of rare marbles, alabaster, and rose windows. Open every day from 7 am to 6 pm with free tours every Sunday at 1 pm, the Cathedral of St. Louis is well worth a visit.

Also in the neighborhood of the cathedral is the plush **Fox Theatre** (527 North Grand). Built in 1929 by movie mogul William Fox, the 4,500-seat theater is what might be called an example of Hollywood-exotic style architecture; it is a mish-mash of styles ranging from Moorish to Far Eastern, from Babylonian to Indian. In its day it was one of the most beautiful movie palaces in the country. In 1982, the Fox was restored and converted into a traditional theater and one of the city's most important performing arts centers, featuring everything from jazz and rock concerts to Las Vegas entertainers and Broadway shows. Tours are available on Saturday mornings at 10:30.

The only remaining original building from the 1904 World's Fair, The St. Louis Art Museum in Forest Park.

The statues adorning the grounds of the art museum, including the forty-seven foot statue of Louis IX of France.

THE WONDERS OF FOREST PARK

West on Lindell Boulevard from the cathedral, or the Forest Park Parkway from the downtown area, is **Forest Park,** the site of the famous 1904 World's Fair and the modern home of a number of fascinating points of interest. The nation's third largest urban park with over 1400 acres (567 hectares) of land (only New York's Central Park and the park system of Portland, Oregon are larger), Forest Park houses a variety of attractions, including the St. Louis Zoo, the 12,000-seat amphitheater called The Muny, the Saint Louis Art Museum, the St. Louis Science Center, the Jewel Box conservatory, and the Missouri Historical Society.

The **St. Louis Art Museum** on Art Hill is a good place to begin. The neoclassical treasury of art sits atop the hill, guarded by an impressive 47-foot statue of the city's namesake, Louis IX of France, depicted in his armor, on horseback ready to fight the crusades. The museum was originally the Fine Arts Palace of the 1904 World's Fair; of the 1,576 buildings built for the fair, the museum is the only one still standing because it was the only one built of permanent materials. The museum, which is considered to be among the country's 10 best art museums, contains more than 70 galleries housing art treasures from around the world and representing more than 3,000 years of civilization. It is also often host to important traveling exhibitions. The museum is open from 1:30 to 8:30 pm on Tuesdays and from 10:00 am to 5 pm Wednesday through Sunday; it remains closed on Mondays.

Only a short stroll through the park from the museum is another family favorite, the Zoo, or the **St. Louis Zoological Park** for those who are picky about names. This leading zoo, for many years run by Marlin Perkins of *Wild Kingdom* fame, is open to the public year-round from 9 am to 5 pm and entrance is free. The Zooline

A family favorite, some scenes of the 83-acre St. Louis Zoo.

Railroad transports visitors around the zoo's 83 garden-like acres of naturalistic exhibits set in reconstructed bluffs and woods, pampas, lakes, and glades. There is, of course, a very good Children's Zoo, a 3.5-acre miniature of the natural world, complete with a nursery for hand-reared young animals. Visit the famous Monkey House and the Bird Cage. Big Cat Country is another must; here are the great felines – lions, tigers, jaguars, leopards, and more – in spacious outdoor homes made as far as possible to resemble their natural habitat. All in all, the zoo is home to more than 2,800 animals, including jellyfish, worms, and insects, all of which can be seen in the brand new *Living World* educational center. Opened in 1989 for educational purposes, the $17 million center is the first such center to combine modern technology and live animals in order to present a unified view of life.

Also in Forest Park is **The Muny,** an institution in St. Louis entertainment. This 12,000-seat amphitheater offers "Broadway's best in the park". There is a little bit of everything at The Muny, from Broadway's most recent hits to the traditional favorites. Attracting the biggest names, this beautiful theater under the stars has become a leader in outdoor musical theater. The Muny's season runs from the middle of June through the end of August.

Still within the confines of Forest Park, on the site of the main entrance to the grandiose 1904 World's Fair, sits the **Jefferson Memorial Building**, which houses the Missouri Historical Society and the **History Museum.** The profits from the fair were used to build the beautiful Neoclassical building and to create the moving statue of Thomas Jefferson. There's at least a taste of just about everything in the History Museum,

On the site of the entrance to the World's Fair stands the Jefferson Memorial Building housing the History Museum.

and a whole helping of a lot of things. The most impressive general exhibits are the colorful ones on the history of St. Louis, the state of Missouri, and the American West. There is an informative audio-visual program on St. Louis from 1764 to the present. The museum also preserves documents and artifacts of the 1904 World's Fair which was of immense significance to the city. The museum's many other exhibits include displays of St. Louis silver work, an exhibit dedicated to volunteer firefighting, another to the pageantry of the Veiled Prophet, and many more. The seemingly endless list of galleries continues with the Old Toy Shop, the Williams Gallery, the McDonnell Aerospace Gallery, the Decorative Arts Gallery, the Gallery of Portraits, and the River Rooms. The museum also boasts an extensive collection of period costumes and period firearms. Perhaps the most fascinating of all, though, is the vast gallery dedicated to Charles Lindbergh. Many of his trophies, medals, awards, and other memorabilia are on display in the Charles Lindbergh Gallery. The museum is open and free of charge all year round, from 9:30 am to 4:45 pm Tuesday through Friday. Guided tours are available by appointment, Tuesday-Friday, just call the Education Department at 361-9265.

Another delightful surprise awaits along a walk through Forest Park toward the McDonnell Planetarium. About half-way between the History Museum and the planetarium lies the **Jewel Box,** a jewel in itself. Built in 1936, this treasure of Art Deco architecture is a step-shaped greenhouse that features changing floral displays. The unique floral conservatory presents an amazing array of flowers and plants all year round. Instead of the usual Muzak, here an afternoon walk through the natural perfumes is accompanied by the musical background of an electric chime carillon. Entrance is free Monday and Tuesday from 9 am to noon; at other times, admission is charged.

The final stop in Forest Park is the **McDonnell Planetarium** and the new **St. Louis Science Center** (formerly the Museum of Science and Natural History) just across highway 40 (Interstate 64) from the planetarium. The planetarium's striking building is another of St. Louis' award-winning pieces of architecture, this one designed by the St. Louis architect Gyo Obata. The recently renovated planetarium now features the Digistar™ computerized projector designed to make the educational features in its 400-seat auditorium even more breathtaking. Also to be found in the Science Center are a number of hands-on exhibits and experiments, plus many displays aimed at both adults and children, on various aspects of physical and natural history. Of special interest for science buffs is the Earth Science Complex which examines different aspects of the land, oceans, atmosphere, and minerals, the Discovery Room, and Science Showplace. Just outside is the Science Park, a brand new concept in outdoor science learning experience. Both the Planetarium and the Science Center are open all year round. The exhibits and parking are free, but there is a small admission charge for the Planetarium and the Discovery Room. For information on hours and show times call 289-4444.

For those whose appetites were whetted by the museums of Forest Park, or for those who are avid museum-goers at heart, St. Louis holds yet more. Among the many historical houses of St. Louis, preserved with period furnishings providing a glimpse into what life was like in times gone by, a few are worth special mention. The **Cupples House** at 3673 West Pine Blvd., justly listed in the National Register of Historic Places, is the 1889 home of Samuel Cupples, a wealthy wood merchant who had this house built with 42 rooms and 22 fireplaces. As one would expect, some of the woodwork is exceptionally fine (open from 10 am to 3 pm Monday through Friday, 2 to 4 pm Sundays). The **Campbell House Museum** is a mid-Victorian townhouse containing all of its original furnishings (1508 Locust Street, open Tuesday through Saturday 10 am to 4 pm, Sundays noon to 5 pm; closed January and February). The **Eugene Field House and Toy Museum** is poet Eugene Field's boyhood home,

In the heart of Forest Park, the Jewel Box conservatory.

Part of the fascinating and informative St. Louis Science Center, the award-winning McDonnell Planetarium.

and what better to do with a childhood home than turn it into a child's dreamland. The house is filled with collections of antique toys and dolls. (634 S. Broadway, open 10 am to 4 pm Tuesday through Saturday, Sundays noon to 4 pm). The **Hanley House** at 7600 Westmoreland offers something a little bit different. This house is a typical Missouri farm house of the restoration period from 1855-1894. Its Greek revival architecture is shared by many farm houses of the epoch. All its furnishings date to the period 1820-1890 (open all year, Friday through Sunday 1 to 5 pm.)

Other interesting museums include the **American Institute of Architects** in the Lammert Building, 911 Washington Ave. Anything to be known about St. Louis architecture can found here (open Monday through Friday from 9 am to 3 pm.) The First Missouri State Capitol is also worth a visit. Located at 208-214 S. Main Street in St. Charles, Missouri, this building served as the state capitol from 1821-1826. The legislative chambers are now fully restored as are two residences and a period dry goods store; hours are Monday through Saturday 10 am to 4 pm, Sundays noon to 5 pm (summer) and noon to 4 pm (winter).

If the weather's nice, nothing could be more enjoyable than a walk through the **Laumeier Sculpture Park** at the corner of Geyer and Rott Roads. One of only two outdoor contemporary sculpture parks in the United States, Laumeier allows for a peaceful walk through the park and provides an ideal setting for taking in some contemporary art. There's also a nature trail and room for picnics as well as a gallery featuring exhibits of contemporary art.

For dog lovers or lovers of the unusual, St. Louis has offerings here as well. The **Dog Museum (Jarville House)** exhibits a rotating selection of works from its permanent art collection and also

The Missouri Botanical Garden in Tower Grove Park is the beautiful home to an astounding variety of plants. Be sure to visit the marvellous Climatron.

has an enormous variety of items depicting the dog throughout human – or canine – history. It can be found at 1721 S. Mason Rd., and is open from 9 am to 5 pm Monday through Saturday, Sundays 1 to 4 pm. There is also the **Dental Health Theatre,** 727 N. 1st Street, with an educator's presentation consisting of 16 three-feet-high fiberglass teeth, films, and puppets; it is open from 9 am-4 pm Monday through Friday, free admission.

Just a short distance southwest of the downtown area is one of the city's most charming and beautiful points, **Tower Grove Park** and the **Missouri Botanical Garden** (Shaw's Gardens). Founded in 1858 by St. Louis philanthropist Henry Shaw, the 75-acre (30-hectare) garden opened to the public in 1860. The garden also administers a 1,600-acre (650-hectare) arboretum at Gray Summit, Missouri, and a tropical extension in Balboa, Panama. Apart from being a very beautiful garden, it is also a place of great educational interest. The park contains more than 11,000 species of plant life, all in a scented and wooded setting adorned by a four-acre lake, islands, footbridges, waterfalls, lanterns, and a Teahouse. The garden's most remarkable feature, though, is the **Climatron.** The Climatron, built in 1960, another award winning structure for its architecture, is the world's first climate-controlled geodesic dome greenhouse. Covered with a plastic skin, it is able to simulate seven different climates and is used to display a wide variety of tropical plants; in fact, it houses more than 4,000 rare plants. Also to be found in the Botanical Garden is the largest traditional Japanese garden in North America. The **Japanese Garden,** or Seiwa-En, "garden of pure clear harmony and peace", is a fourteen-acre island of tranquillity. From Memorial Day through Labor Day the garden is open from 9 am to 8 pm and for the rest of the year from 9 am to 5 pm; admission is $2 for adults, $1 for senior citizens, and free for children

The Missouri Botanical Garden.

Washington University stands out among the many institutions of higher learning in St. Louis, not for its academic reputation alone, but also for the beauty of its campus.

under 13. You can also take a two-dollar tram ride around the park.

More than just a center of industry and commerce, St. Louis has a deep-rooted tradition of higher education. The first university founded west of the Mississippi is here in St. Louis. It is **St. Louis University,** founded by the Jesuit order in 1818, and still considered one of the nation's leading Catholic universities. **Washington University,** founded in 1853, is nationally known and has hosted 18 Nobel laureates, five of whom did their Nobel Prize winning research at the university itself. Both the University of Missouri and the Southern Illinois University maintain growing campuses in St. Louis. Those who are planning a visit to Washington University should be sure to stop by the **Washington University Gallery of Art** (Forsyth at Skinker). The first art museum west of the Mississippi River, it was founded on May 10, 1881, and was known as the St. Louis School and Museum of Fine Arts. This institution later gave birth to the City Art Museum (now the St. Louis Art Museum) and the Washington University facilities now go by the name of the Gallery of Art and the School of Fine Arts. Thus, to sum up, it seems fair to say that St. Louis has something for everyone, as might be expected from a thriving city with a metropolitan area of 1.2 million people. From the many attractions of its renovated city center to its many shopping and convention possibilities, St. Louis is an oasis in the expanse of Middle America.